Let's pretend maths

Resources Centre

Helen Williams

Acknowledgements

Our thanks to children and teachers at:
Baring Primary School, Lewisham
Holy Trinity and Saint Silas CofE Primary School, Camden
Ridgeway Primary School, Croydon
St George the Martyr CofE Primary School, Camden
Chris Wright, BEAM consultant

Special thanks to:
Julia Bond, Primary Adviser for Early Years, Cornwall
Debbie Byrom, Family Services, Cornwall
Helen Bromley

Published by BEAM Education
Maze Workshops
72a Southgate Road
London N1 3JT
Telephone 020 7684 3323
Fax 020 7684 3334
Email info@beam.co.uk
www.beam.co.uk
© Beam Education 2006

ISBN 978 1 9031 4238 7
British Library Cataloguing-in-Publication Data
Data available
Edited by Marion Dill
Designed by Malena Wilson-Max
Cover photo by Len Cross
Photographs by Chris Wright, Len Cross and Ken Wilson-Max
Printed in England by Cromwell Press Ltd
Reprinted in 2008.

Contents

Foreword

Recently, I came across an article in the *Times Educational Supplement* about American early years educationalist Vivian Gussin Paley. Her new book *A Child's Work* had been published that week, and I bought it. Vivian Gussin Paley has been an early years teacher for over 30 years. An author of 11 books, she believes in the critical role of fantasy play in the development of young children. In her inspirational *Wally's Stories: Conversations in the Kindergarten* and the later *A Child's Work*, she describes a model for making fantasy play happen. Her model involves the telling and reading of stories – read and reread, told and retold again and again. She observes the children playing, asks questions to draw out the narrative of their play and invites them to 'tell the story' of their play. These stories are then acted out, with the storyteller choosing their cast. As the stories are told, the narrative develops and becomes more complex. It is this model that I had in mind when writing this book about role play.

So where does the maths fit in? I think the best place to start is with what mathematics is and what mathematicians do. Mathematics takes place in our heads. It is a mental and a social process, a language we use when interacting with each other. It is about properties, relationships and patterns.

An ability to function mathematically is one aspect of human functioning – we all do it. I mix play and maths for expediency. There is no doubt young children will play even if I don't want them to! So why not use this to generate some maths? We can make sure they focus on mathematics by being aware of the mathematical opportunities that our play scenarios present. This book will help you recognise these. The children can hardly help but engage in mathematics – they will be surrounded by it!

Helen Williams

Chapter 1

Mathematics in role play

"Mathematics is not only taught because it is useful. It should be a source of delight, wonder and excitement and an appreciation of its essential creativity."

National Curriculum Guidance, DfES

Mathematicians experiment, invent, describe, conjecture, guess and visualise. In short, they use mathematics to solve problems. All these characteristics of mathematics can be observed in young children as they play. As a child pushes a selection of shapes through shaped holes, they try out different possibilities, guessing and visualising, experimenting with various shapes, selecting a likely shape and discarding shapes that do not fit, twisting and turning shapes to see if they fit.

As children engage in mathematics at school, we need to nurture their natural capacity to act as mathematicians from the very beginning while they learn to count and calculate, recognise shapes, and so on, before they can 'become' mathematicians. We do not become mathematicians by learning something that is called mathematics, or numeracy, but by doing mathematics the way in which it is created or applied outside school: by acting as mathematicians from the start.

By 'acting as mathematicians' we ask children to

- describe *What can you see? What can you say?*
- explore *I don't know. What do you think?*
- invent *What are you going to try now?*
- experiment *I wonder if …?*
- recognise patterns *Can you see what comes next?*

- conjecture *I wonder what would happen if ...?*
- guess *Do you have any idea whether ...?*
- visualise *What would you see if ...?*

Children actively seek to understand their world. The question is, do we make good use of this in our mathematics teaching? How do we encourage visualisation and imagery which are integral parts of mathematics? By visualisation and imagery I mean something much broader than 'mental arithmetic': the ability to 'see' something, to think what is, or what might be, going to happen before doing something – to predict. For example, I could fold a piece of paper in half and then in half again. Imagine I cut off the corner. What shape will the hole be when the paper is opened out? Can you describe what you 'see'? How do you know?

The world of mental imagery is based on our perception and experiences. Play provides a wealth of experiences for children to draw on when they visualise. In addition, while we engage in fantasy play, we picture others and ourselves in a range of situations. It is important for young children to engage in visualisation and discussion in playful situations in order to be able to use this skill in a structured way in later mathematics.

And what about story and role play? What does that have to do with mathematics?

Storytelling is a fundamental human activity. Every day we hear, read and tell stories: "This morning, I was just about to leave for work when the postman caught me ..." Through stories we both make sense of our lives and present ourselves to others.

'Pretend' and fantasy play are rich in problem-solving contexts. Stories of all sorts – stories from books, from television, from families and friends – nourish children's ideas. Young children weave stories into their lives, moving seamlessly between fantasy and reality. The skill for us as teachers is to find interesting mathematical problems that hook the children. Stories can be an invaluable source of these: "One day, Little Red Riding Hood got lost ... what did she do, do you think?"; "But when Grandpa turned up at the travel agent's, it was shut."

When I am finding it difficult to get a young child to start something, I often use 'pretend': "Pretend we are going to count these shells – where shall we start?" It seems to release children to begin. When we pretend, we hold an idea in our mind that is not (yet) real – a hypothesis that can be explored intellectually. When we pretend, we do not have to be afraid of being wrong. We can experiment with confidence. For a while, I had to pretend I was writing this book!

One common problem with mathematical teaching and learning is over-concern with correctness. Young children sometimes are unable to make a start on something because they do not want to be wrong. Think how accessible mathematics is without this fear. Allowing children to choose the way the 'story' of the role play unfolds means there are no right and wrong answers, and yet we can still introduce some challenging mathematics for them to engage in.

Role play is rich in opportunities to use and to record maths for a purpose, to use authentic tools and to select the appropriate tools for the problem: "We need some stamps – how shall we remember which ones we need?"; "How can we find out if this parcel will fit in the letter box?"

When young children play with their maths, they too experiment, invent, describe, conjecture, guess and visualise. Learning is interactive: children actively construct their understanding within a social and physical environment. Well-planned play, particularly role play, provides numerous opportunities for interactive learning to take place.

For children as learners, the benefits of a mathematically rich role-play environment are

- first-hand experiences presented by the play, opportunities for children to both listen and be heard, to work collaboratively and to use their imagination – "Did you hear that? What could it be?"

- space and time to experiment, try out their ideas and problem-solve.

The teacher listens with care, rather than dominating or jumping in too quickly.

Emerging mathematical skills can be supported by pretend play by using role-play props accumulated over time to simulate real life and help children generalise from what they have learnt in one situation to another. This is a key way that children consolidate and extend their mathematics learning – from knowing how to count out a requested number of pennies from a large pile to selecting the correct number of coins from a purse full of mixed coins to pay for a pizza in the classroom 'takeaway'.

Enriching role-play areas with mathematical artefacts such as calendars, calculators, clocks and telephones offers children the possibility of engaging in maths activities and conversations about numbers as they discuss possible dates for birthday parties and outings and press buttons for telephone calls.

Identifying the mathematics

We aim to be creative from the children's perspective. We know what we want to cover over the year: purposeful counting, calculating, data collecting and recording, problem solving in terms of measures and shape and space; and lots of mathematical discussion, language and vocabulary development. We then link the role play to the maths by identifying questions to ask that reflect the maths focus, such as: "How big will the basket need to be?"; "How many sandwiches will you need to pack?"; "What do you think Bear's favourite food is?"

There are generic story problems that lend themselves well to using some mathematics, covering the entire curriculum, and all role play will provide opportunities, to lesser and greater degrees, for mathematical content.

These specific story events, for example, generate mathematical problem solving:

- There's been a robbery ... *How much? Is that all of it? How do you know?* (counting and calculating)
- I've lost my money ... *How much?* (counting and calculating)
- The bus is late ... /The doctor is delayed ... *What time will it/ they be here? How long do I have to wait?* (measuring)
- We are lost ... *What shall we do? How shall we find out way?* (measuring; understanding shape and space)

Keeping focused on maths

Before setting out to engage children in role play and explore the world of maths, we need to exploit the maths opportunities within the early learning goals and prepare for role play to incorporate these. Here are some examples:

Mathematical symbols

Numerals as labels – bikes and parking bays numbered, a list of telephone numbers next to the telephone

Counting out beans for the bears beans factory

Numerals as amounts – '2 thermometers' on the vet's thermometer box

Numerals as prices – fruit and vegetables labelled with their prices in a shop or market scenario

Mathematical tools

Tape measures, scales and weights, clocks, calculators, calendars

Mathematical problems

Identifying the problem: "How much can I get into this box/these suitcases?" Providing a range of sizes of boxes/suitcases to pack with various items.

By using role play and storytelling, we nurture children's capacity to think and to problem-solve, and we enrich the mathematical possibilities, just as mathematical inputs, problems and events enrich the play.

In addition, it is helpful to balance the time we explore mathematics in a role-play context, and the time we engage in mathematical discussions with children, based on what we see and hear. In these discussions, the adult and the children

Explaining the result of a game

work together to develop an idea, and we ask questions to encourage children to recap ("So, what happened after that?"), explain ("Why do you think Lucy said that?"), to predict and reflect ("I wonder what would happen if ...").

In this book I have identified activities that develop and explore maths in particular role play contexts, you will find these ideas in *Lets do maths!* boxes.

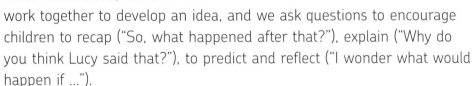

Let's do maths!

- Write or draw a dry-cleaner's price list.
- Make laundry tickets to give to customers.
- Put together a collection of coins for the washing machines and dryers.
- Set a kitchen timer to the correct drying times for the laundry.
- Measure and weigh different amounts of washing powder.
- ...lothes into piles...

Observing and assessing children's learning

Role play offers ample opportunities for children to apply all their developing skills, including their mathematical knowledge and understanding. Our role is to observe whether children take an active part in the play and engage in the mathematical discussions, and our assessments need to focus on the following:

Recall and knowledge

Observe the depth of knowledge children are bringing to the play

What knowledge are children displaying about the context?
Are they using and responding to numerals and numbers?
What use do they make of mathematical equipment?
What counting and checking skills are children using?
What previous mathematical experiences are they making use of from home or school?
What are they drawing from the story?

Observe how the props are used

Is there one prop that is creating more interest?
Are children selecting/using tools appropriately? Or are they using what is available rather than what they need?
What understanding of the tools are children showing?
Are they demonstrating knowledge of numbers? Which numbers?
Are they organising and distributing materials?

Talk and collaboration

Observe and note the degree of interaction

This is important as role play depends upon children learning to interact with others to solve a problem.

Is there a lot of silence?
Are children playing in company, but independently?
Are they playing in partnership with anyone for any length of time?
Are children listening to what others say? And adjusting their play as a result?

Observe the language and conversation

Discussion and explanation are critical in mathematical problem solving.

Are children explaining or describing to one another?
Are children using any mathematical language and vocabulary?

What range of vocabulary are they using?
Informal and/or formal?
Are they having any authentic discussions/conversations?

Involvement and motivation

Observe involvement

Without willingness to become involved, children are not going to apply themselves to solving mathematical problems.

Children can use and apply mathematics 'hands-on' at a market stall or car-boot sale.

How long do children play there? Do they choose (not) to play there?
Are they absorbed? What are they focusing/concentrating on?
How confident/knowledgeable do children appear in the scenario?

Initiative, creativity and interests

Observe interests

This sows the seeds to develop the play.

Are there any original ideas?
What new elements are children introducing into their play?
What are they interested in?
Are there any interests that could lead to incorporating mathematics?

These could comprise recognising and using numerals, counting and calculating, data handling and organising, constructing and building.

We should not worry if many of the mathematical opportunities seem repetitive and make use of similar mathematical content. Children not only like repetition – think how often they enjoy hearing a favourite story read over and over again – but gain mastery and confidence at an aspect of mathematics by repeating things a number of times. Also, each time, the context for counting and calculating, for example, will alter and allow children to use their skills and knowledge in a slightly different situation.

At a later stage, we will be interested in seeing what children use of the mathematics they have been taught, observing how they apply what they have learnt in one situation to another.

Based on these observations, it is possible to fine-tune role play and give it a solid 'outer' structure, within which children explore playing and learning maths to their individual abilities and at their individual pace.

Chapter 2

Children's pretend play

"Role play is one way of getting children truly excited about learning and applying what they have learnt to their everyday life."

Early Years practitioner

Role play and pretending

Role play and pretend play – play where, for periods, the participants are walking in another's shoes, where they are acting out a role within a scenario based on something that happened in real life, on a storyline from a book or a tale or on a fantasy image – can provide many of the experiences and interaction necessary for children to make sense of their

world. High-quality pretend play sometimes involves quite complex negotiations between pretenders and gives children experience of being in charge of their lives. While children pretend and role-play, there will be innumerable opportunities for them to apply all their developing skills and knowledge. This will include a lot of joint planning and problem solving as well as using and applying mathematical skills, knowledge and concepts. The joy of role play is in contributing to the discussion and being part of the action.

There are two key elements to effective pretend play:

Make it real and make it work

For example, a shop needs a house to bring the shopping home to; a post office needs to deliver its letters and parcels somewhere. What sense does a child make of a situation where they 'shop', being asked to pay attention to the correct amount to pay, then having to replace the items on the shelves when their 'turn in the shop' is finished? To make it work, the shopping must be done for a purpose, albeit a pretend one.

Give it time

Pretend play needs extended time to develop to a high level of complexity. Children also need time to familiarise themselves and experiment with the environment and the resources, and they need time to try out things. Early experiences, both alone and in groups, should be free and uninterrupted. Structure is then necessary for children to create and develop roles and for us as teachers to draw out the mathematics, to challenge and to stimulate and support. We need to spend time modelling behaviour and roles so that we offer new experiences. Not every child will know what to do when they go into a café or a florist's as a customer, let alone as a member of staff.

The role-play area

Role play does not necessarily need a large, dedicated area. Four posts or broom handles cemented into four buckets make a good role-play framework on which to hang drapes and paper. If space is at a premium, you can easily store a range of relevant props and 'costumes' in a suitcase or box. In addition, having a shop set up nearby as well as a house means you can involve larger numbers of children at a time, without the need for space elsewhere.

The location of the role-play area can make a big difference. I have included ideas in this book for moving the role play out of doors, for making it bigger and more active and for extending the traditional home corner wherever possible.

It is beneficial to involve children in both the design and construction stages of the role-play area and the home corner as this will help 'ownership' of the area. Engaging children in setting up the area, resourcing it and putting things away at the end of the session is a valuable process for identifying with the role-play action, for being part, for belonging.

As an extension to a role-play area, you can introduce linked stories and related activities. For example, if you have chosen a journey-type story for a role-play scenario, you could elaborate on the theme by suggesting children pack things for a picnic on the way. You could establish a picnic

The farmers' market – a different way of setting up a shopping experience.

site in the outdoor area and provide all the usual picnic paraphernalia such as a blanket or tablecloth, baskets, plates and food.

The home corner

The home corner is distinct from the role-play area, although a small setting may not have room for both all the time. The role-play area sets up situations from daily life outside in the world: fire station, travel agent, hairdresser, dentist, building site, airport, restaurant, and so on. The home corner has furniture and props that might be found in a home: bed, sofa, washing machine, kitchen table and cupboards, and so on.

The secret here is that we need to think of everything appropriate to young children that takes place in a home somewhere and think of the maths that is inherent in that environment. We can then resource discrete packages that will stimulate children's real-life and fantasy play to include mathematical activity. Children don't include maths in their role play automatically – one research study found that the children they observed hardly use any maths in independent play. It is worth spending time watching for this and noting what provision stimulates mathematical behaviour as much as possible.

We will need to model mathematical behaviour for the children in everyday homely events and use mathematical language and talk in a day-to-day way, and we will need to structure some adult-led activity to present maths in a home-corner context before children will incorporate these ideas in their play.

One way of doing this is to take out elements of the home corner as a separate, adult-led activity, then reintroduce these into the home corner with the same mathematical structure. For example, offer children a separate activity where they dress up three different-sized dolls. Children select the clothes that match the size of the doll and dress the doll, in discussion with you. Or set up a telephone and mobile phone activity, with children inventing their own telephone directories and personal telephone numbers. Then, at a later stage, put all these resources in the home corner and observe whether children apply what they have learnt in the activity to their play.

The routine of tidying up the home corner is an opportunity for building in mathematical experience such as matching, lining up and organising. For example, children can fit shaped objects to silhouettes, count out the right number of implements to be stored in each labelled pot and fold up clothes to fit into drawers and cupboards.

The home corner can also be outdoors. Set up a tent with all the provisions for living. The size of the space will be different, with the furniture and implements on a smaller scale. Have a giant's home with big boxes for chairs and large plates and mugs.

A role-play area can be time-consuming to set up from scratch each time, but some form of home corner is essential for the youngest children to explore their ideas and concerns. If this is removed and replaced with the 'post office', they will often still play 'house' and 'mummies, daddies and babies'. Older children may have grown beyond the house and use the space to explore being a superhero.

Try introducing a garden next to the home corner or gradually building a 'mini community' by adding an area to visit from the 'house', such as an office or shop. Experiment with variations on the house theme: living in a caravan, a tent or being on holiday in a chalet.

Choosing a theme

As teachers, we can offer an alternative viewpoint, encourage further thinking or clarify an answer, but, ultimately, we work with the children's suggestions. Open-ended problems allow all children to access the mathematics with their varying knowledge, abilities and skills.

The themes we choose for role play need to be appropriate to children's ages and stages of development. We also need to consider issues of gender and cultural diversity. The role-play area and the home corner have to make sense in terms of children's experience: a vet's surgery, for example, will not have much meaning for a child without a pet. It helps if children are involved in deciding the theme of the area. This will reflect their current interests, and almost all themes allow for some mathematics to be introduced.

We should also choose themes that make a positive and stimulating contribution to children's speech and language development. Bilingual learners as well as children with particular needs may require longer, free and uninterrupted play experiences to allow them to develop and create suitable roles and characters and to try out things.

Adult play alongside is helpful in modelling behaviour and speech – for example, 'thinking aloud' such as: "Oh dear! My dog is poorly! I think his tummy hurts, because he hasn't eaten his dinner … I must phone the vet. Where did I write down that number?"

Initiating and developing role play

Pretend play can start anywhere spontaneously. We have all experienced the situation where artefacts take on a life of their own and where young children seemingly involved in constructing something can suddenly pretend a brick is a phone and start to have an extended telephone conversation with the brick held to their ear.

The following dialogue illustrates this further. Lily is sorting out Cuisenaire rods, holding two of them and talking in two different voices:

Lily, holding the 3 rod in one hand	*I'm very, very small, and you're very, very big.*
The 10 rod held in the other hand replies	*I'll look after you, little girl, 'cos I'm very big and tall.*

A conversation on size and 'looking after' possibilities continues for a few minutes until Lily decides the pretend is over and the rods are returned to the box.

Or take the following conversation about a robbery in a flower shop: joining in the role play as an interested onlooker at a later stage can help focus children on potential ideas for mathematics while continuing to develop the play

Liam (shopkeeper)	*These cost 2p. Toni, what do these cost?*
Toni (shopkeeper)	*1p.*
Ashleigh (customer)	*I've spent my 1p.*
Aaron (customer)	*Somebody's got my money.*
Ashleigh to Aaron	*Is this your basket?*
(Liam is on the telephone.)	
Toni	*Where's the money gone? I've lost my money … Oops, I haven't lost my money, it's in my hand.*

Liam	*Lovely flowers!*
Aaron	*Someone's stole my money!*
Toni	*I've got £100 in mine.*
Ashleigh	*I'll ring the police for you,*
Aaron	*Where's the phone? I need to ring the police.*
Ashleigh (on the phone)	*Burglars come and stolen Aaron's money. Bye.*
Aaron to Liam	*Someone's stole my money!*
Ashleigh to Aaron	*No! He's the burglar!*
Liam	*I've got just 1p ... 5p ...*
Aaron (on the phone)	*Police, please ... Oh no! The police are here.*

This conversation is an opportunity to do some counting and calculating. Talk with the children to develop the idea:
Have you lost your money? I'd like to know more about what happened ...
I wonder how much has been lost/stolen? How can you be sure?
Is that all of your money? Or some of it? How do you know?
What shall we do now?

Then clarify the problem:
OK, Aaron, we need to know exactly how much you have lost so we can check it when we find it.

Make a suggestion:
Aaron, write down how much has been stolen to show the police when they arrive.

At the end, arrange for some real money to be 'found' and counted:
Look what's there under the table! It must have fallen out of your pocket! How much is it? Let's count!

Props and resources

An important part of developing play is involving everyone in collecting, displaying and discussing suitable props and resources over time for both indoors and outdoors role play. This can be, for instance, a brainstorming event, with the children suggesting what they would need to set up a café. Props, for example, for role play based on a classic storybook like Pat Hutchins' *Rosie's Walk* (HarperCollins, 1968) would be the story landmarks (pond, hutch, and so on) labelled 'in the farmyard' for children to find their way around as well as notices, maps and routes around the farmyard drawn by the children. Arrow signs could include such things as 'three pigs live here' and 'underneath the fence'. This would ensure that children have opportunities to use lots of mathematical positional words and number words, but they could also contribute their own knowledge and experience of other stories about farm animals.

Not all resources need to be authentic: sometimes less is more, as too many props can overwhelm young children. For example, show children a feather as a prop and see where their imagination takes them.

To change the role play's original direction, introduce a new 'event' such as: "Guess what! When Rosie got up this morning, the farmhouse gate was open! What do you think might happen today?"

You can also enhance the play by including appropriate music or sounds.

One of the best ways to introduce or reinvigorate the role play is a visit to a place that relates to the story, visits from people whose characters or occupations appear in the story or simply telling or reading a story, followed by discussion about what was said and done, and why. This is particularly important for real-life and apprenticeship contexts.

If a visit to a particular place is not an option, you may want to consider showing children a video of such a place.

Introducing a story chair

Another supporting feature of role play is a 'story chair', where children sit when telling their stories after they have played in the role-play area.

We can invite children to the story chair to tell their story, tape-record the story or use their words to make a book, and we can encourage listeners to ask questions of the storyteller.

This can be an opportunity to develop an aspect of the story into a mathematical discussion or a chance to set up a problem-to-be-solved debate.

A 'story chair' is an extending feature of role play.

A fairy story box.

Small-world and story-box play

Setting up small-world and story-box play after a role-play session helps children re-enact and recreate on a smaller scale what they have been doing previously. It is a further means to recap on the maths experienced during role play. Children can reuse most of the props and resources for the role play, albeit in a smaller size.

All the mathematics that can be drawn out of role play can also be drawn out of pretend play with small-world artefacts. Small-world play literally gives children a different perspective on the problem and the scenario. It provides a smaller, safe space for children to play and experiment with ideas 'unwatched' and often less distracted. It is easier for them to control all the characters, unlike during role play. They become the producer of the whole story and control the action. Children may work through ideas that had their beginning in role play, which they can then integrate into their next role-play session at a later stage. Using small-world play that is linked to the role play helps children explore their ideas creatively.

Story boxes

Story boxes are 'small worlds' – themed settings created inside a box. The stories are as many and as varied as the different children or adults who open the box. They are whatever the storyteller or pretend player wishes the story to be. Story boxes are not to be confused with story sacks – large cloth bags with a storybook and supporting materials.

Story boxes become effectively a 'small-world role play', and it is powerful for children to move between the two experiences. Like role play, story boxes are open-ended, put together to encourage many different stories to emerge from the same theme, wherever the children's imagination takes them. It is the children who choose the way the story unfolds. This, in turn, opens up all kinds of possibilities for posing mathematical problems by both the children and the adults once time has been invested for free and uninterrupted play.

Imagination is essential to mathematical problem solving. Story boxes provide opportunities for discovering children's interests, language development and mathematical understanding (for example, counting how many dinosaurs would fit in the valley or for how many guests the table has been laid), for foreseeing next steps – and for being amazed by what children already know!

In addition, story boxes can easily be taken home to provide a link between child, school and home.

Here are examples of story-box themes to be used with young children in a mathematically stimulating context:

Story-box theme	Contents	Maths learning
Camping out	Hankies made into tents and sleeping bags Play people Tiny bags and boxes Miniature plates and cutlery	Order and sequence events Count out objects from a larger group Share plates and cutlery
Fairy box	Different-sized fairies Fairy beds and chairs Small mirrors Sparkly counters Different-sized stars Wizard figure Selection of wands and small crowns	Order sizes Show an interest in number problems
On the road	Drawn road system Road signs Bridge Pond Vehicles Play people	Use common shapes to build models Describe journeys and respond to directions and instructions Use positional language
Party box	Birthday cake Candles and holders Invitations Party hats Birthday cards Cups and straws Plates Presents Birthday banner Birthday food	Recognise numerals Share objects into equal groups Wrap presents
Treasure box	Pirate or play people Treasure map Jewels and gold bars Treasure chest Trees Sand Small spades	Find the total number of objects in two groups Use positional language

Using ICT to enhance role play

Any role-play area we resource should include a range of ICT equipment. At times, we may want to station a computer in the role-play area: such scenarios might be an office with the computer or laptop to be used for writing letters and collecting data, a doctor's surgery or hospital for patients' records and prescriptions. On other occasions, we include a mobile phone, a calculator, stopwatches and timers. The home-corner area could be equipped with a microwave cooker and TV remote control. And reflecting on role play is always supported by using a digital camera and a webcam.

Problem solving through role play

Children learn to solve problems by recognising there is a problem and understanding what it is about, by being systematic and by being persistent. We can help by

- providing a rich mathematical environment with challenges
- recognising and exploiting the problem-solving potential in a range of contexts
- creating an atmosphere where exploring in order to solve a problem and 'having a go' at a solution is seen as more important than getting the answer right
- talking, talking and more talking.

Supporting children who are reluctant role players

Some young children may be more comfortable in solitary play or in parallel play where two or three children play alongside each other, but do not communicate at all. You can develop the play towards more social pretend play by encouraging older peers to join the 'group' of solitary and parallel players who are likely then to direct the play and give the reluctant ones a role or a task, albeit a lowly one: "You be the baby, and I'll be the Mummy"; "You be the assistant and do the sweeping, and I'll be the owner." In this way, the less social players will be able to talk about what happened and contribute to any later maths discussion about rotas for tasks or whether there were enough brooms for all sweepers.

Tempting children into the role play by hiding an interesting prop in the area and challenging them to find it can also work as can offering a 'tiny bit of pretend' to draw someone in: "Pretend I am holding a cup ... here it is. Here you are, take it from me. Can you go and put it on the table over there?"

My experience shows that it hugely depends on the theme chosen if children are reluctant to take part. Ask yourself: "What interests do children have? Would they like a garage as a role-play area? A car wash? A cave or camp?" Ask them!

It is beneficial to involve children in both the design and construction stages of the role-play area and the home corner as this will help 'ownership' of the area. Engaging children in setting up the area, resourcing it and putting things away at the end of the session is a valuable process for identifying with the role-play action, for belonging.

Another idea is to gather a group of children in the role-play area or home corner for a story, a chat or an informal discussion – it could become a place to sit and talk together as well as a place to play. Even children shy to participate will be curious enough to 'see what it's all about' and will, eventually, join in.

Chapter 3

Real-life scenarios

"At the dry-cleaner's. we've got big, big machines, and you put your dirty clothes in and they come out all clean and folded up small."

Grace, 4, during role play as manager of a dry-cleaner's

Real life offers a plethora of ideas for role play. In this day and age, even young children are familiar with a variety of places and everyday situations that lend themselves to being acted out in a playful way.

Mathematical apprenticeship role play provides the chance for children to learn new skills, language and vocabulary and is a key way children can consolidate and extend their mathematics learning enjoyably.

Apprenticeship role play is also rich in problem-solving opportunities: using and recording mathematics for a purpose; using authentic tools (tape measures, scales, money) and selecting the appropriate tools for the problem; describing and explaining; predicting and visualising what has happened, what will happen and what might happen if certain events change direction. While engaged in apprenticeship role play, young children are learning many critical things in addition to mathematics, mostly associated with the behaviour patterns and vocabulary particular to that scenario as well as to how to relate to and communicate with one another.

What's the maths in real-life scenarios?

Role play based on real life is the classic 'mathematical' play. Whether in an office or a shop, times and written records are kept, payment is exchanged for goods or services, and comparisons are made as items are checked, counted and maybe weighed and measured. Here, the provision of mathematical tools such as clocks, calendars and diaries will support a richer discussion about times, dates and appointments.

For young children, such play will focus on the following:

Main mathematical idea: Number	Example: A visit to a café
Sorting, organising and categorising, handling data	Setting up the café, laying out knives and forks, taking a customer order
Counting reliably and comparing quantities	Serving meals, delivering the correct number of sandwiches and drinks
Reading and recording numbers	Writing a food order, making a telephone call from a listed number, reading the menu, sitting at numbered tables
Recognising coins and exchanging money for goods or services	Paying or taking payment, giving change
Solving practical calculation problems	'Families' of two or three ordering and paying as one, working out what is left at the end of the day and needs ordering when the café closes
Talking about time	How long and when is the café open? Do we have time for another drink? How long will it take to be served?

Forward planning

Good-quality mathematical learning will not happen easily if we don't plan for it to happen. To make play effective mathematically, we first need to give the children time to become engaged in the scenario. The early play should be free and uninterrupted, allowing children to find their way around, to establish roles, to explore resources and to try out ideas. Routines and ways of engaging have to be established: "How many can play here? When can we play here? What should we do with the things after we've finished?"

Main mathematical ideas: Measures, shape and space	Example: The shoe shop
Measuring length Comparing sizes and shapes Making pairs	Measuring feet, fitting shoes, sorting shoes by size into different-sized shoe boxes, labelling small, medium and large shoes
Flat and solid shapes	Matching shoes to shoe outlines on shelves
Describing position and direction	Giving directions on the telephone to the shoe shop or another shop
Making a price list	Drawing up a list of shoe prices
Reading and recording numbers	Writing out cheques, explaining the use of credit cards and how a till works, sorting coins

Our first job at this stage is to make sure that children will 'stumble over' some mathematics – for example, always including a working clock, a telephone book and a calendar by the telephone, a calculator as well as a note pad and pens. Such 'mathematical apparatus' stimulates initial play and discussion.

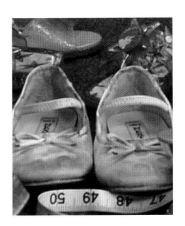

We have to model behaviour and roles – talk the talk and walk the walk! The role play will not develop without such input from us: some children may know how to order flowers over the phone or respond to a customer entering the café, but many may not. Children will have a range of experiences of the adult world. Providing role models helps apprenticeship play become both effective and extended and bring the 'real world' into a setting.

Role models can come from

- a visit to a location such as a launderette, post office, garage, small supermarket (café, takeaway, shoe shop, clothes shop, greengrocer's, an open-air market or bazaar), where the children can observe and where real people talk on site about what happens at their location

- a visit from someone after or before a planned outing to discuss their occupation (park attendant, estate agent, deep-sea diver, miner, chef, mechanic, travel agent, bus/taxi driver, nurse, firefighter)

- watching a video taken in a relevant scenario, with time for discussion on what the children saw happening.

Afterwards, it is important to help children reflect on the visit, the visitor or the video and discuss the roles of the different characters:

Why do people go to a launderette?
What can you do at a post office?
Why do people visit garages?
What do they do when they get there?
Who works at a vet's? What do they do?

Setting up the role-play area

Involve children in setting up the role-play area and the home corner. Ask them to help find appropriate resources for both: a shop needs a house to bring the shopping home to; a post office needs somewhere to deliver the post.

Appropriate props make the mathematics come alive. Good equipment will contribute to the quality of play. Introduce new props and remove old ones as time goes by to add new stimulus and avoid overwhelming children. A balance of child-made and authentic props is best – for example, a real foot measure as well as one made by attaching a tape measure to a sheet of cardboard. However, it is a good idea not to compromise on items such as weighing scales, clocks and calculators, which should be working, and money, which should be real. Real coins look and feel correct, and it is difficult to see how a young child can begin to identify different coins without using 'proper' money. Tell

children that they are going to use real coins, and they will look after them. Put a coin check sheet as a lining in the till drawer section - use a photocopy of each coin. Children can check as staff when the shop closes.

An excellent problem-solving task for children is to price items or services and it is a useful way for us to assess easily what understanding they have of numbers and values. Whether children can recognise coins and identify their value depends on their experience with real coins and real shopping. It is unrealistic to have items priced in pennies. Many children are well aware that very little can be bought for a penny or even 10p. Unless you have opened a pound shop or hold a jumble or car-boot sale as shopping opportunities, it is more realistic to price in whole pounds – this way, children are still dealing with whole, smallish numbers.

You can use many of the resources or props again in different scenarios. Keeping a list of mathematical props and accessories for each scenario is efficient and will save time in the long run.

A model: The launderette and dry-cleaner's

All role-play scenarios can be based on the following model and modified accordingly.

Opening a launderette and dry-cleaner's provides an ideal context for combined play and mathematical problem solving, both indoors and outdoors. Clothes will need to be checked in and out, sorted, washed, rinsed, dried and ironed, folded, packaged and returned to the correct owner.

Setting it up

Role-play area and props:
Reception desk, working clock, telephone, telephone directory; laundry lists, raffle tickets to attach to laundry items, receipt book; till with real coins, calculator, calendar; ironing board and iron; large cardboard-box washing machines and dryers, airers, laundry baskets, clothes hangers on a rail; waiting chairs and magazines, signs and prices ('Special offer this week', 'Hand-washing 20p per item', closing and opening times); cleaning materials, chart of washing symbols/instructions; name badges for staff; audio tape of washing noises.
Introduce these props over time.

Outside role-play area:
Washing line, pegs, bowl for hand-washing, buckets; different-sized bags/boxes to transport washing; range of clothes in the home corner; purses with money and safety carrier bags.

Getting started

Start with
* a visit to a launderette taking some washing or
* a visit from someone who works at a launderette or
* watching a video taken at a launderette or dry-cleaner's

Customers visit the launderette with bags of washing, either doing their own washing or leaving it for a set period of time for a service wash.

Maths learning
Describing, explaining and predicting
Recognising and using numerals
Recognising coins
Ordering events
Using the vocabulary of time and duration
Using the vocabulary of measures

Involving children
Why do people go to a launderette?
What do they do when they get there?
Who works there? What do they do?
What might happen here?
How do your clothes get washed.?

Laundry ticket	
Name	
Item	Amount
Trousers	
Shirt	
Dress	
Pants	
Socks	
Collection time	

'Real' telephone arrangements can be made, visits kept in 'real time' and fitted in with other home events ("Do we have time to go to the launderette?"), and we have to consider what washing to take and how to get it there ("There's a lot of washing today – what shall we carry it all in?").

Becoming involved

Teacher's role:

❖ Make a telephone call to the role-play launderette that begins a mathematical discussion. Model the conversation by involving the children listening as you telephone a member of the launderette staff who sits with their back to you. This models more accurately a telephone conversation as the speakers cannot respond to facial expressions or gestures.

Hello. My washing machine is broken. What can I do? Can you help me? When can you fit in a service wash for me today? What do I have to do?
How long will that take?
What time shall I come back?
What will it cost?

❖ Visit the launderette with your washing and join in the play. Ask questions to invite mathematical discussion:
What coins do I need for this machine?
How long does the dryer take?
How much powder is best?
How long does it last?
I am not sure if this blouse should be washed or dry-cleaned. Can you help me?
What about the label? What do the various symbols mean?
When can it be collected?
Can you write me a receipt?

At the end of the session, you may invite children to sit in the 'story chair' (p21) to tell their story about what happened at the launderette today.

Let's do maths!

❋ Write or draw a dry-cleaner's price list.

❋ Make laundry tickets to give to customers.

❋ Put together a collection of coins for the washing machines and dryers.

❋ Set a kitchen timer to the correct drying times for the laundry.

❋ Measure and weigh different amounts of washing powder.

❋ Sort clothes into piles of light- and dark-coloured clothes.

❋ Make a change machine.

❋ Collect and sort pictures and photos showing how to save water.

❋ Make a display of different-sized containers for water (washing-up bowl, cup, jug, and so on).

❋ Use 10 dried beans to make rain sticks with empty kitchen-roll tubes and tape.

❋ Peg out numbers on an outdoor washing line.

Observations and assessment

Start by spending five-minute intervals sitting nearby and noting what happens, who is in which role, some of what is said, what takes place. This will help you plan what to do next, not only for mathematics but for all other areas (see also p11, chapter 1).

Do children

- take an active part in the discussion?
- describe what happened, using a range of appropriate vocabulary?
- retell some events in order?

Discussion time

The questions in *Discussion time* should relate to what the children have been doing in their role play.

What might happen here?
Who went to the launderette today?
What did you bring with you?
When did you go?
Can you explain what you will do first ... second ... next ... last?
When you play here, who do you want to be?
Can you describe what happened, Dan? What did you do?
How long did you stay there today?
Rema, pretend you are working at the launderette – what would you say to Sonny about his big bag of washing?
What character would you like to be next? Why?

Small world and story-box play

Create a story-box launderette. Contents may include: play people, bowls, mop or similar, miniature washing machine, scraps of material for clothing, washing line and pegs.

Link the outside builders' yard with an indoors warehouse.

Maths learning

Describing and explaining

Comparing sizes

Comparing shapes

Using the vocabulary of position and direction

Using the vocabulary of shapes

The building site

Brainstorm, ask building experts and look in books to identify the machines which help builders build houses and other buildings. Mention screwdrivers, hammers, nails, saws, drills, cement mixers, bulldozers, steam shovels and pipe diggers. Talk about different tools and how to use them safely and emphasise using safety goggles, thick gloves, hard hats and heavy boots.

Set up a space in the outdoor area for children to develop as a building site. Make sure that it is coned or roped off from the rest of the outdoor environment and is big enough for large-scale investigative play with ramps, planks, bricks and wheelbarrows. These materials provide opportunities for children to use different shapes to investigate rolling, sliding and gradient. Children will also need space to build large-scale structures and be able to use the wheelbarrows to transport different materials. Also provide an office space for the 'site manager' with desk, computer keyboard, calculator, diary, calendar and other office equipment.

Setting it up

Role-play area and props:
Protective clothing, including hard hats, goggles, overalls, thick gloves, reflective strips, tools, tool belts, tool aprons, tool-carrying bags and boxes; measuring instruments, including long tape rule, trundle wheel, wheelbarrows, collections of bricks (wooden, large plastic, some real bricks) and bags of sand, trowels, a large spirit level, shapes, range of different-sized pieces of wood, nails and hammers; block-and-tackle equipment and buckets in various sizes.

Talk about the need for a site office and discuss the resources needed for it with the children. Look at plans and architects' drawings.

Getting started

Start with

❋ a visit to a building site or a building observation point or

❋ a visit from someone who works on a building site

Discuss with the children what they know about building and their experiences of building sites. Share ideas about foundations, scaffolding and building materials such as bricks, tiles and wood.

Involving children

Who knows what happens on a building site?

What do the people do who work there?

What clothes do you have to wear on a building site?

What tools would you use on a building site?

Make a collection of house bricks for the children to examine closely and feel. Look at the shapes in the bricks and take measurements. Talk about edges and corners as well as the different faces of the bricks.

Discuss with the children building a brick wall, look at the patterns of bricks at the nearest brick wall and how it is built. Talk about what holds the bricks together. Use spirit levels and plumb lines.

Observations and assessment

Do children

- offer a solution to a problem?
- recognise and use numerals and counting in their role play?
- use a range of mathematical vocabulary?

Discussion time

I wonder how we can find out how long the wall is?

What do you think would happen if we didn't build the wall straight?

What's the best way to put mortar on a brick?

Can you find anything else that is as heavy as a brick?

How can we check that we have laid more than two bricks each?

I can't decide if Teddy could see over the top of the wall or not. What do you think?

If you stretched your arms really wide, do you expect that you'd be able to touch both ends of the wall at the same time?

Let's do maths!

- Together make up some real mortar, measuring out sand, cement and water. Use real bricks and trowels to make a low brick wall.

- Construct different shapes, joining together pieces of wood, using hammer and nails.

- Use recycled materials on site to create a large 3D structure.

- Write a work plan or timetable, saying who can be on site and when.

- Draw building plans and take site photographs.

- Measure and sort different lengths of wood.

- Make a collection of different-coloured bricks and experiment with colour mixing to get different brick colours.

- Paint rectangles and discuss the effect of sprinkling spoonfuls of sand on the wet paint to represent the roughness of brick.

- Transport different-sized buckets of sands, using block-and-tackle equipment.

- Price and sell building materials.

Small-world and story-box play

Create a story-box building site with sand, miniature bricks and wooden sticks so children can make a scaffolding. Further contents may include: play people, buckets, miniature tools, cranes, bulldozer and similar vehicles.

Real-life scenario ideas at a glance

At the airport

Setting it up

Role-play area and props:
Check-in desks ('Long Distance', 'Short Haul'), telephones, working clocks, calendars; check-in list of passengers, luggage labels and stickers, scales, suitcases, tape measure, bags, tickets in number order; passports, newpapers, magazines, books; hats, uniforms, name badges for staff; tape recorder for announcements; aircraft cabin outline drawn on the floor; chairs with numbers on.

Getting started

Start with
* a visit to an airport or a terminal or
* a visit from someone who works at an airport or
* watching a video taken at an airport

Passengers check in at a check-in desk, have their luggage labelled and weighed, have their passports and luggage checked, look at flight departure list and board an aircraft.

Maths learning

Reading numerals

Reading and comparing prices

Ordering events

Weighing

Exchanging money for goods

Using the vocabulary of time and duration

Maths learning

Reading numerals

Reading and comparing prices

Sorting and categorising

Exchanging money for goods

Calculating

Let's do maths!

* Make numbered tickets for the passengers at the check-in desk.

* Weigh the suitcases. Which is the heaviest/lightest?

* Measure the length and the width of each suitcase and bag.

* Provide a large digital clock made by the children and write a list of flight times.

* Write luggage labels with destinations and distances.

* Create your own passports, recording details of height, age and address.

A car-boot sale

Setting it up

Outside role-play area and props:
Box of coins, purses/wallets and money; carrier bags, tables and boxes; a range of items to sell (left-over knick-knacks from the school fete, clothes, Christmas cracker toys, and so on); receipt pads, calculator, labels/stickers, opening sign.

Getting started

Start with
* a visit to a car-boot sale
* a visit from someone who runs a stall or
* a discussion with children on who has been to an outdoor sale

Stallholders set up their stall and price their items. The beauty of a car-boot sale is that items can be priced under £1. Customers buy from a range of stalls, negotiating price reductions and checking change. Bought articles are either displayed in the home corner or resold on another stall.

Let's do maths!

* Write price labels for the goods to be sold.
* Sort goods in various groups.
* Sort money by value into separate pots.
* Draw a plan of the car park and show the position of each stall.
* Write notice boards for the opening and closing times of the car-boot sale.

At the vet's

Setting it up

Role-play area and props:
Reception desk, working clock, appointments diary, pet-record cards, calendar, calculator; till and coins, price list of treatments, chequebooks, paper and pens, appointment reminder cards; surgery table, different-sized pet boxes, different-sized soft toys (pets), white coats and badges for surgery staff, stethoscope, bandages and doctor's bag/equipment; weighing balances, bathroom and other scales; measuring tapes.

Maths learning

Reading numerals
Using measuring words
Using the vocabulary of time
Weighing

Let's do maths!

* Use a computer to fill in details of your 'pet', recording its name, age and weight.

* Construct a pet box for your pet.

* Measure your pet and write a food diary.

* Make an appointment with the vet.

* Write a rota for vets and assistants, saying what time they will be on duty.

Getting started

Start with

* a visit to a vet's surgery or

* a visit from someone who works at a vet's surgery

'Real' telephone arrangements can be made, appointments kept in 'real time' and fitted in with other home events; home visits can be made to extra large or poorly pets. Pets – transported safely – might have to remain overnight. Pet passports can be written for each soft toy, and children can decide on the cost of treatment and how to pay.

Maths learning

Reading numerals

Describing, explaining and predicting

Comparing sizes

Using the vocabulary of position and direction

Using money words

Bicycle repair depot

Setting it up

Outdoor role-play area and props:
Appointment diary, pens and pencils, telephone, calculators, swipe cards and machine, cash register and money; overalls and caps; spare tyres and wheels, spare inner tubes, sticky squares or plasters to mend punctures, tools for removing and replacing tyres from wheels; bowl of water, chalk, bicycle pumps, pressure measures.

Getting started

Start with

* a visit to a car tyre or bicycle repair centre or

* a visit from someone who works at a tyre centre or bike shop

Set up a bicycle service centre with a reception area and bays for parking and working on bicycles, trikes or scooters.

Talk with the children about experiences of having a flat tyre on a bicycle or a car and discuss changing wheels and tyres. Introduce the various

Let's do maths!

* Turn bikes and a pedal car upside down and describe what happens when the pedals go round.

* Put numbers in order on the bikes and cars that come in for repair.

* Set up a system for writing estimates, quotes and invoices for repairs.

props and talk about how they might be used. Look at all the moving parts and find out what they are all for. Describe the tools needed to mend a puncture on a bike.

Discuss the sort of services that the 'Quick Fit Wheel and Tyre Centre' could provide and how much they might cost. Make some labels, advertising the services on offer and their cost.

When the service centre is open, children take turns in checking the wheels on the bikes and trikes and checking that they turn well. They can work with inner tubes, using pumps and pressure measures. Remind children that when the centre closes, everything needs to be left organised for the next opening time.

Going on safari

Setting it up

Outdoor role-play area and props:
Tent or material stretched over a washing line; outdoor camping furniture such as table, chairs, sleeping bags; mosquito nets and camouflage material; tin plates and cups, washing-up bowl; a supply of binoculars, magnifying glasses, pooters, cameras and rucksacks; a range of protective clothing for different weather and terrain expeditions; animal identification charts; bag of decorative bark to replicate forest ground.

Getting started

Start with
❋ a visit to a wildlife centre or zoo or

❋ a video of a safari park and African animals

Invite the children to help you set up a safari centre. Together put up the tent and ask for ideas on what it might be like living in a tent or outside. Discuss with the children what sort of animals they might see when they are on safari. Encourage them to talk about the wild animals they would recognise, using animal identification charts. Decide what to pack into the rucksacks to take on safari.

Let's do maths!

❋ Estimate and count how many animals there are.

❋ Sort the wild animals by size.

❋ Use twig arrows to lay trails to follow.

Chapter 4

Storybooks and picture books

"An adult reading aloud to kids is the best thing ever. Other people's imaginary worlds spinning around in your head help you create your own."

Jacqueline Wilson, writer and 4th Children's Laureate

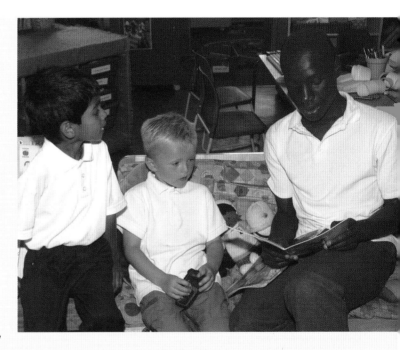

Storybooks and picture books are visual treats and narrative masterpieces, playing an essential part in a child's intellectual and emotional development.

To develop the pretend play problem solving, we may want to consider using book-based stories as a context for doing some mathematics. Almost any story can be used for mathematical problem solving. If the maths is not immediately obvious in a storybook, look for opportunities to use the story to introduce maths-related resources such as coins or timetables, to use a range of measuring equipment, to move from place to place and give directions and to make telephone calls to arrange events and collect data and information.

When a character from a storybook or picture book series becomes established, use the scenarios or situations that the character is involved in as a starter for a role-play area. When you have decided on a certain theme such as losing things (which is a recurring scenario in many picture books), you and the children can set up a role-play area called 'Lost Property Office'. You will need to decide the 'real-life' maths that is likely to occur in that area and then talk to the children and together make sure that the appropriate resources are there.

What's the maths questions for story and picture books?

Counting and understanding number

Count, read, compare and order numbers:
How much ice cream do we need? How many beach balls did you pack? Can you fetch three buckets? What can we write down to remember that number?

Calculations

Combine groups of objects and take some away:
How many will there be if we add three more? What if we take two away?
I wonder if there are the same number of mugs and plates? How can we find out which there are most of?

Data handling

Sort and match objects, make choices and justify decisions:
Do we need more? Have we got enough? How can we find out? Is it too small or the right size?

Measures

Compare lengths, weight and capacity:
How heavy is the shopping? Which bag is lighter, this one or that?
Which one did you decide was the tallest? Does anyone know how to use a measuring tape?

Shape and space

Describe location and direction:
I spy something without any corners ... it rolls. What shape will we get if we cut these sandwiches in half?
I wonder where we find the kiosk. Do you happen to know how to get there?

Here are examples of storybooks and ideas for combining role play with maths:

Storybook	Role-play area	Maths learning
Susanna Gretz/Alison Sage: **Teddybears Go Shopping** (A&C Black, 2000)	Supermarket or shop	Counting Calculating Measuring
Pat Hutchins: **We're Going on a Picnic** (Red Fox, 2002)	Outdoors	Counting Calculating
Jez Alborough: **It's the Bear!** (Walker Books, 2004)	Outdoors	Counting Comparing sizes
Judith Kerr: **The Tiger Who Came to Tea** (HarperCollins, 1968)	Café	Counting Sharing Using money
Janet and Allan Ahlberg: **The Jolly Postman** (Viking, 1986)	Post office	Numbers Sorting Ordering events

Story world: Grandpa and Thomas

Pamela Allen's book *Grandpa and Thomas* (Viking Children's Books, 2004) tells the story of a young boy going on a beach picnic with his grandfather. The general themes are 'relationships', 'outings' and 'journeys'. Picnics and journeys, in particular, allow us to explore the following mathematical topics: numbers (counting how many items); measures (length and distance – how far; time – ordering events, how long in duration) and shape and space (describing where you are – location; how you get there – direction).

Thomas's journey is a safe journey, with familiar events taking place. As the narrative develops, we can introduce 'what ifs' and additional characters with problems to solve, and there will be further opportunities to encourage mathematical discussions about distances, costs and time.

Any of these ideas can be adapted and used with other outing/journey stories. What is important is what interests children.

Through the train window we saw a.....

Maths learning

Describing, explaining and predicting

Counting

Ordering events

Organising

Categorising

Comparing distances

Comparing duration

Using money

Using the vocabulary of time

Using the vocabulary of position and direction

Setting it up

The scenario for *Grandpa and Thomas* ideally needs to be set up outdoors or, for reasons of authenticity, you may want to consider taking the children on a picnic or outing to the park or beach. The home corner, in this case, could be Grandpa or Thomas's house. Introduce a linked place for the characters to visit, for example a 'beach' in the outdoor area. You can easily create a sand area outside by laying thick plastic or pond liner on the ground and covering it with sand and small pebbles to represent the beach. Encourage the children to remove their socks and shoes and wriggle their toes or make and count footprint trails in the sand. Have patches of damp sand as well as dry sand. Provide large umbrellas so that the sand can be used on sunny or wet days.

Outside role-play area and props:
Big picnic rug, smaller tablecloth, bag with picnicware; buckets and spades; flags and feathers for sandcastles, large collection of shells and pebbles; sunhats and sunglasses.

Getting started

Start with

❋ reading the book together with the children. If possible, tape-record the text so that children can listen to it several times.

Discuss the story with the children and ask if have they been on a picnic themselves, talk about what happens when you go on a picnic and what you need to take with you. Encourage children to think about places where to have a picnic and tell the group what happened when they went on a picnic.

Involving children
Who has been on a picnic?
Where did you go?
How did you get there?
What did you take?
Why do you like picnics?
What's special about picnics?

Becoming involved

Teacher's role:

❖ Model making a telephone call to 'Grandpa' to see at what time he is going to pick up Thomas. Check how many sandwiches and biscuits need to be packed and how many utensils are necessary for building a sandcastle.

When will the two of you leave?
How many bags are you going to take? What's inside those bags?
How will you get to the picnic area?
Do you think six sandwiches will be enough for the day?
Why do you need three different-sized plastic buckets?

❖ Start with "Can I come with you on your picnic today?" and join in the play.

Where are we going?
How long will we be gone?
When is it time for lunch? I'm hungry!
What do I need to bring?
What shall I do to help?
What have you decided to pack for our picnic today?
Is it far?
Are we there yet?

❖ Encourage children's natural creativity and ideas by starting the session 'with a twist': "One day, Thomas and Grandpa set off for the beach, but when they opened the front door ... it was raining! What do you think might happen next?" Organise a real picnic in a local park with food and activities.

At the end of the session, invite children to sit in the 'story chair' (p21) and to retell the story in their own words.

Observations and assessment

Do children

- take an active part in the role play and ensuing discussion?
- describe what happened, using a range of appropriate vocabulary?
- retell the story in a sequence?

Let's do maths!

* Make, cut and eat real sandwiches.

* Pack cups, saucers and plates into picnic baskets so that they fit.

* Rehearse laying out a picnic, using a tablecloth and cutlery.

* Provide orange-coloured water and a selection of jugs, bottles and plastic mugs to fill and empty.

* Together collect information on children's favourite picnic food and display it as a chart.

* Vote for where to go on a picnic: the beach or the park.

* Write a 'what to take on a picnic' information book, using drawings and photos.

* Draw a map of how to get to the picnic area.

* Estimate and count how many minibeasts you see on the picnic.

* Make a picnic zigzag counting book: 1 tablecloth, 2 baskets, 3 flasks ...

Discussion time

Where did you go today?
Can you tell us how you got there?
How long were you going for?
Ruby, pretend you are Thomas – what would you say to Grandpa?
What character would you like to be next? Why?

Small-world and story-box play

Line a shoe box with sandpaper and add blue cloth for the sea. Contents might include: play people, squares of cloth for picnic rugs, picnicware, buckets and spades, tiny flags, feathers, shells and pebbles, shark or boat.

Fill a play tray with sand, shells and appropriate small-world toys for children to recreate the story.

Story world: Duck in the Truck

Maths learning

Describing, explaining and predicting

Counting aloud

Ordering events

Using the vocabulary of position

Duck in the Truck (HarperCollins, 1999) is one of a series of picture books by Jez Alborough featuring animal characters: Duck, Sheep, Goat and Frog. The stories are written in rhyme, with repetition and humour both in the words and the illustrations.

Setting it up

This story is best recreated in the outdoor area, where children have space to move around.

Outside role-play area and props:
Use pedal cars and stick cut-out boat shapes to some of them so that children can rehearse being Duck or Goat driving about in a truck or a boat. Include road signs and direction signs made by the children.

Getting started

Start with

❄ reading the book together with the children

Discuss the story with the children: when and where do they themselves go in a car? Has anyone ever been on a truck? Ask children where they may have seen the characters 'for real':
on a farm in the country, a city farm, at a petting zoo or in the garden pond.

Involving children

Have you ever been on a long journey?
Where did you go?
Why did you go?
How did you get there?
What did you take?

Becoming involved

Teacher's role:

❖ Invite the children to help you build Duck's truck. Use resources such as large plastic crates, wooden community blocks and recycled cardboard containers.

Do you think this truck is large enough? Does it need to be larger or smaller?
How many passengers will fit in?
How fast can the truck go?
Where does it stop?

❖ Together collect artefacts that Duck might need in his truck. Show the children a toolkit and discuss what the tools might be used for.

What do you think this tool is used for? Do you know what it is called?
Can you think of a tool that could be used instead?

❖ Ask children if you can sit in the truck with them and go on their next journey.

Where are you going?
When will we arrive there?

At the end of the session, you may invite children to sit in the 'story chair' (p21) to tell their story about what happened in the truck or on the boat today.

Observations and assessment

Do children

- predict what could happen next?
- give reasons for why something happened?
- order events?

Discussion time

How would you have help Duck get out of the muck? Where did you go today? How did you get there? How much time did it take? What character would you like to be next? Can you explain why?

Let's do maths!

- ✳ Draw some maps for Duck to keep in the truck.
- ✳ Be car mechanics and mend Duck's truck.
- ✳ Use thick string and tie some knots in case Duck's truck needs towing.
- ✳ Sort out Duck's shopping and stow it in the truck.
- ✳ Help Duck move the truck by experimenting with 3D solids, deciding which ones roll and which ones slide.

Small-world and story-box play

Use a play tray filled with sand and gravel and resource with small cars, trucks and plastic animals.

Create a garage in a small box. Contents might include: play people, animals, miniature cars and trucks, miniature tools, small pots of colour, buckets, cloth, telephone.

Let's do maths!

- ✳ Do a stocktake of the repair centre: count how many screw drivers, hammers and nails there are. Decide together what other items need counting.
- ✳ Draw silhouettes and labels for each item.
- ✳ Give invoices to owners of mended objects.
- ✳ Set up a clock and watch mending outlet, using numbers and clock faces to support the 'menders'. Sort out the watches that need repairing.
- ✳ Supply a large diary and write down the repair jobs for the day.

Using the same character to develop the role play

Another book in the series about Duck and friends is *Fix-It Duck* (Harper Collins, 2005). In this book, Duck engages in DIY jobs such as stuck windows and leaking roofs. This is a good jumping-off point for setting up a repair workshop where children can rehearse being mechanics, carpenters and builders.

Story world: Look Out! It's the Wolf!

In the delightful *Look Out! It's the Wolf!* by Emile Jadoule (Zero to Ten/Evans Publishing Group, 2004), the wolf, for once, is not the bad guy but a much-loved friend of Mr Deer, Rabbit, Pig and Bear. This is not obvious from the start, though (unless you look closely at the illustrations), and while reading the story to the children, there will be mounting suspense as the wolf is on his way to the house where his friends are waiting for ... the wolf's surprise birthday party! Mathematical topics here include numbers and the number system; measures and shape and space.

Maths learning
Describing, explaining and predicting
Counting
Making patterns
Ordering events
Using measures
Sorting

Setting it up

The final scene for *Look Out! It's the Wolf!* is the secret birthday party that the other animals have been preparing for Wolf, and the obvious place to site it is the home corner. Children will be delighted to be involved in decorating the house for a secret birthday party, much as it happens in the book itself. You could encourage the children while they are all busy decorating to keep looking out for the wolf and say when they see him. You could provide wolf ears for children pretending to be the wolf.

Getting started

Start with

⚜ reading the book together with the children

Discuss the story with the children, talk about any parties they had been involved in or been to as a guest. Some children in the group might not celebrate birthdays, so you might choose to put the emphasis on 'party' rather than on 'birthday'. Ask children when in the story they realised there was going to be a birthday party and point out that you didn't know until the very last page. Read the story again and together look at the illustrations and identify where you can see the other animals getting ready for the party.

Involving children
Have you ever been to a party?
How do guests know what time to arrive?
Were there lots of guests at the party?
Are parties always in people's houses?
When would you have a party?

Becoming involved

Teacher's role:
Invite the children to help you make a list of the things that are needed for a party. Together identify where these things can be found or bought.

How can we find out how many plates and cups we will need?
How many cartons of juice do we need?
What colour balloons shall we buy?

At the end of the session, invite children to contribute to a 'how to organise a party' zigzag book.

Observations and assessment

Do children

- predict what could happen next?
- give reasons for why something happened?
- order events?

Let's do maths!

- Sort out a collection of birthday cards with ages on and wrap up lots of 'presents' in different-coloured wrapping paper.
- Make and decorate party hats.
- Thread material triangles on string to make bunting.
- Cut out pairs of animal ears to wear to the party.
- Make jelly in different-shaped containers.

Discussion time

What present would you buy for a special person?
Which one of the animals would you invite to a party?
What shapes can birthday cakes be?
How would you feel if someone did a secret party for you?
What age do you think Wolf is?

Problem solving in storybooks

Most storybooks can be used for mathematical problem solving. Some storybooks have a particular mathematical theme as part of the story that you can use as a focus, alongside more general problem solving.

Problem solving with number:

Title	Author	Maths focus
The Paper Bag Princess	Robert Munsch	An interest in numbers
The Shopping Basket	John Burningham	Sorting out a shopping list and the number of things on it
Mrs McTats and Her Houseful of Cats	Alyssa Capucilli	Adding one more
The Doorbell Rang	Pat Hutchins	The problem of sharing with an increasing number of guests

Problem solving with time:

Mr Wolf's Week	Colin Hawkins	Days of the week
Time to Get Up	Gill McLean	Days of the week and the time of day
What's the time, Mr Wolf?	Colin Hawkins	Time of day
Bear About Town	Stella Blackstone	Days of the week

Problem solving with shape and space:

The Quilt	Ann Jonas	Pattern
The Patchwork Quilt	Valerie Flournoy	Pattern
My Cat Likes to Hide in Boxes	Eva Sutton/Lynley Dodd	Shape and size of boxes

Problem solving with measures:

Jim and the Beanstalk	Raymond Briggs	Size, scale and the need to measure
The Smartest Giant in Town	Julia Donaldson	Size and scale
Pardon? Said the Giraffe	Colin West	Height
Who Sank the Boat?	Pamela Allen	Size and Weight
Mr Archimedes' Bath	Pamela Allen	Capacity

Problem solving with money:

Don't Forget the Bacon	Pat Hutchins	Shopping
The Great Pet Sale	Mick Inkpen	Selling
A Chair for My Mother	Vera Williams	Saving money
Bunny Money	Rosemary Wells	Spending, change

Chapter 5

Traditional tales

"The first was the great big bear, the second was a middle-sized bear, and the third was a little teeny tiny bear."

Goldilocks and the Three Bears

Telling and reading traditional tales is a powerful way to help children listen, talk about and discuss ideas. Unlike storybooks, traditional tales do not have an agreed text. Traditional folk tales encompass many of the play themes explored by children far and wide and over many years: power and struggle against power, heroes and villains, jealousy and pleasure, friendship and safety, growing up and separation. These are important emotions for children to explore in a safe environment.

Many traditional tales start with everything being fine, then something happens in the middle, and often the main character is helped out by another character before everything is resolved by the end of the story.

Help children use their imagination and make connections with their everyday lives. With the retelling of traditional tales, the storyteller has the opportunity to influence the content by adding more characters and changing the ending.

Many of the old tales have stories about three characters and involve counting as part of the plot. Most traditional tales are good, simple stories that can be used as a basis for a role-play area and dramatic play. They also offer a rich seam of mathematical problem solving and opportunities for mathematical discussions. While some stories are well suited for counting, others are good for talking about the size of things or for discussing the patterns that are created. Most of the stories have events that take place in a set order which children remember: this means that you will hear children talking about time and when things happen.

What's the maths questions for traditional tales?

Counting and understanding number

Count, read, compare and order numbers:
How many are there? Who knows what that number is?
I wonder what number comes next? Let's all count together.
How could you find out what the number 6 looks like?

Calculations

Combine groups of objects and take some away:
How many will there be if we add one more? What if we take one away?
How many are there altogether? How many are left?

Data handling

Sort and match objects, make choices and justify decisions:
Do we need more? Have we got enough? How can we find out?
How can we find out how many there are?
How will we remember where you went?

Measures

Compare lengths, weight and capacity:
Does it fit? Is it longer than the mat? Does it feel heavier than the shoe?
How can we find out which one's the longest?
What do you think will happen next?
Is it too small or the right size?

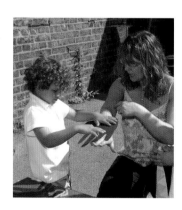

Shape and space

Describe shapes and make patterns:
Can you see another shape like this one?
I wonder what is missing from the pattern?
Can you describe where you found it?
What would happen if you go underneath?

In addition to mathematical themes, the following traditional tales contain certain recurring generic story problems:

- Getting lost
- Does it fit?
- Do I have enough?

Story	Role-play area	Maths learning
The Gingerbread Man	Kitchen	Shape
Three Billy Goats Gruff	Outdoors, bridge	Size and pattern
Goldilocks	The three bears' house	Comparing sizes
The Three Little Pigs	The pigs' house	3D structures
Jack and the Beanstalk	The giant's castle	Size and counting beans
The Great Big Enormous Turnip	Outdoors, in the garden	Putting things in size order
Little Red Riding Hood	Grandma's house	Planning routes
The Elves and the Shoemaker	Shoe repairer and shoe shop	Counting and doubling
Cinderella	Cinderella's kitchen	Size, shape and time
The Wolf and the Seven Little Kids	The little kids' house	Counting animals

Little Red Riding Hood

Little Red Riding Hood, a traditional tale by the Brothers Grimm, provides a strong context for exploring the goody/baddy relationship as it brings together the elements of safety and danger. Once children know the story well, suggest that they play around with it, making the main character a boy with a blue hood or changing the story ending.

Setting it up

In the classroom, *Little Red Riding Hood* is easy to set up in the home corner. As the narrative develops, introduce a linked place for the characters to visit: this could be Grandma's house or the wolf's lair.

Maths learning

Describing, explaining and predicting

Counting

Ordering events

Sorting

Organising

Using the vocabulary of position and direction

Role-play area and props:
Grandma's house, one bedroom, each suitably furnished; working clock, telephone, notepad and pens, calendar by the telephone, shopping-list board in the kitchen; calculator, walking stick, glasses, apron, suitable jewellery, slippers, watch, handbag, purse, real money.

Outside role-play area:
Use curtains and screens to make a second home area, the house of Little Red Riding Hood, so that children can make journeys between the two houses. Make sure that the route between the houses is signposted and has objects on the way for the wolf to hide behind.

Getting started

Start with

❋ telling or reading the story

Telling this familiar story gives the whole group a shared experience and focus. It allows you to use gestures, voice and facial expression as well as to interact with the children. Children will listen to the repeated words and phrases, and you will notice them using them during their play. Introduce one or two simple props and use these when telling the story – for example, a basket and a walking stick. Alternatively, you might want to use puppets or soft toys to help tell the story.

> **Involving children**
>
> *I wonder what's going to happen next.*
> *Who do you think this belongs to?*
> *What do you think this is for?*
> *Where do you think they met?*
> *How do you think the story will end?*

While you are telling the story, use phrases that are part of storytelling such as: "Once upon a time ..."; "In the beginning ..."; "One day ... Next ... And ever since then ..."; "And they lived happily ever after ..."; "The end". Using these 'time' and sequence words helps children get a sense of the progress and passage of the story.

Becoming involved

Teacher's role:

❖ Ask the children what they could do to turn the home corner into Grandma's house. Discuss with them what would be different about a grandmother's house to their own. Collect artefacts with the children and arrange them in the home corner.

What things were mentioned in the story?
Will Grandmother need a chair? Can you explain why you think that?

Will she need a table? How do you know?
How long will her bed need to be?
What might happen here? Who will come here?
How do you think she felt when … ?
When you play in here, which character do you want to be? What will you do?

❖ Tell the children that you are going to make a telephone call to Grandma: "I tell you the numbers, can you type them in for me?" Model the conversation by having the group watch as you call Grandma, who sits with her back to you:

I was just about to go to the shops … I can drop in on my way back …
Is there anything you would like me to get while I'm there?

❖ Visit Grandma's house with a present for her and join in the play:

Hello! How are you today? I thought it would be nice to bring you a gift.
Have you had any other visitors today? Yes, please, I'd love a cup of tea.

At the end of the session, you may invite children to sit in the 'story chair' (p21) to tell their story about what happened in Grandma's house today.

Observations and assessment

Do children

- take an active part in the discussion?
- describe what happened, using a range of appropriate vocabulary?
- retell some events in order?

Discussion time

What did Grandma/Little Red Riding Hood do today?
Why do you think that happened? What might happen next?
Simon, can you pretend you are Grandma – what would you say to Little Red Riding Hood?
How can you get to Grandma safely?
How long did it take you to get from your house to Grandma's house?
Which was the heaviest/lightest item in the basket?
What character would you like to be next? Why?

Let's do maths!

- Sort and weigh the items to be put in Little Red Riding Hood's basket.
- Invent and write down telephone numbers for Grandma and the wolf.
- Measure the distance from Grandma's house to the wolf's lair.
- Use strips of paper to make a collection of body measures.
- Use pipe cleaners to make different-sized spectacles for Grandma and the wolf.

Small-world and story-box play

You can explore the *Little Red Riding Hood* story further with small-world toys, a story box or puppets.

Create an indoors room in a small box. Contents might include: play people, wolf, red material for a cloak, bed, scraps of material for bedding, chair, door, basket, cakes, flowers, and so on.

Alternatively, children turn the story-box into a forest.

Goldilocks and the Three Bears

Maths learning
Describing, explaining and predicting
Counting
Ordering events
Sorting
Making patterns
Using the vocabulary of size
Using the vocabulary of time and duration

Another popular story to use for Foundation Stage maths is *Goldilocks and the Three Bears*. This story gives children a chance to compare big things and little things and to put objects in order of size, so a lot of activities around this tale centre on sizing, matching, sorting and sequencing. Goldilocks is ideally suited for children to talk about what happens first and what happens next and to work things out in their heads.

Setting it up

Convert the role-play area into the three bears' house. To develop the potential maths learning, equip the area with three different sizes of all the resources, especially the important ones such as bowls, spoons and chairs. Have a notice on the outside of the role-play area that says 'The three bears' house' and change the usual way into the house: you could put the doorway on the other side or change the height so that children have to stoop to get into the house. Introduce a linked place for the bears to go to – a bear school where the bears go to learn bear basics.

Role-play area and props:
Two-room house, one kitchen, one bedroom, each furnished with three different-sized beds and chairs, table; different-sized bowls, plates, spoons, porridge pot.

Outside role-play area:
Invite the children to set up a playground for the three bears in the outdoor environment. This could be the climbing apparatus or you could use any other swinging or balancing equipment.

Children can draw and follow maps to the bears' playground, describing position and giving and receiving directions.

Getting started

Start with

❈ telling or reading the story

Telling this popular story gives the whole group
a shared experience and focus. It allows you
to use gestures, voice and facial expression and to
interact with the children. Introduce two or three
simple props and use these when telling the story –
for example, three different-sized spoons or bowls
to demonstrate comparison.

> **Involving children**
>
> *I wonder who sleeps in the largest bed?*
> *Who do you think this belongs to? Why?*
> *Why do you think these objects are different sizes?*
> *Where do you think the bears went?*
> *How long did it take them to get there?*

Becoming involved

Teacher's role:

❖ Introduce the bears' house. Draw children's
attention to the different sizes of the things
in the house and discuss why this might be.

Emphasise words such as 'small', 'smaller',
'smallest' and 'long', 'longer', 'longest'.

*Whose house do you think this is? Can you explain
why you think that?*
*Who lives here? Whose bowl is this? How do you
know?*
What might happen here? Who will come here?
How do you think the bears felt when ... ?
*When you play in here, which character do you want to be? What will
you do?*

❖ Invite children to look for or make other artefacts that are three
different sizes to resource the bears' house. Discuss with children what
lengths and sizes of pencil and paper the bears might use and collect
together a bears' library of different-sized books and brochures.

*I've bought some catalogues because I thought the bears might want
to order some new furniture, china and beds. Can you choose some?*

❖ Visit the bears' house with three wrapped presents and join in
the play:

*Hello! I've bought the bears a present each, but I've lost the labels, so I'm
not sure which present is for which bear. Will you help sort them out?*

At the end of the session, you may invite children to sit in the 'story chair' (p21) to tell their story about what happened in the three bears' house today.

Observations and assessment

Do children

- sort objects according to size?
- notice patterns developing?
- use a range of appropriate vocabulary?

Let's do maths!

* Make collections of soft toys and order them by size.

* Draw pictures of the three different-sized bears.

* Put the spoons and bowls in the correct order, starting with the smallest.

* Measure and use construction material to build three chairs.

* Lay a breakfast table for the three bears.

Discussion time

Why do you think Goldilocks went to the woods in the first place?
What time of day do you think it was? Why do you think that?
How could she find her way?
What did the bears do today?
Why do you think that happened? What might happen next?
What animals other than the bears could be in the story?
How long do you think Goldilocks stayed in the bears' house?
Which was the smallest/largest item she saw there?
What can you see from the bears' house? Is that tower on top of the hill or behind it? What else can you see?
Where else could the bears live?
Suppose there were four bears! Where would the 4th bear fit in order? Is it a cousin? A grown-up bear?

We're going on a bear hunt....

Small-world and story-box play

You can explore the *Goldilock and the Three Bears* story further with small-world toys, a story box or puppets.

Convert a small box into an indoors room. Contents might include: play people, bears, beds, scraps of material for bedding, chairs, bowls, plates, spoons.

Support the children in retelling or developing the story, using the props and commenting on their sizes, and ask appropriate questions:

I wonder what happened after Goldilocks went home?
Do you think the three bears were happy?
What would you have done to help them?

Jack and the Beanstalk

An English fairy tale from the 18th century, *Jack and the Beanstalk* presents young children with a heady mix of magic (magic beans! golden eggs!) and simple maths. The story is perfect for combining role play and mathematics, with plenty of ideas within the story to investigate further.

Setting it up

Build a giant's castle together with the children. Explain to them that everything in the castle needs to be of gigantic proportion. Many everyday artefacts can be used to resource the castle, such as large plastic washing-up bowls as porridge bowls and a large towel as a face flannel, with a small handbroom as a toothbrush. As the narrative develops, introduce a linked place for the characters to visit – Jack's house or the farmers' market, where Jack sells the golden eggs.

Role-play area and props:
Adult-sized table and large chair; huge book; washing-up bowls for breakfast dishes and serving spoons as teaspoons; large calculator and A3 sheets of paper for writing calculations, broadsheet newspaper; large golden coins made from sprayed metal jar lids.

Maths learning
Describing, explaining and predicting
Counting
Weighing
Comparing height and size
Using the vocabulary of position and direction
Using the vocabulary of time and duration

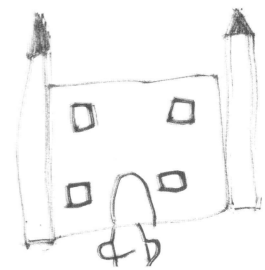

Outside role-play area:

❖ Garden, gardening tools, watering can, plants, dried beans, large stone to sit on.

❖ Playground with a giant handprint chalked onto a wall or the ground.

Start the playground scenario as follows: "During the night, we had a visit from the giant. Look at the size of his hand!" Children measure the print with rulers, tape measures and string. They then share their findings and the methods and strategies they used for measuring.

Why do you think the giant came to visit?
How did he get here? How long did he stay?
How often would your hand fit into the handprint? Can you guess before you start measuring?

Getting started

Start with

❀ telling or reading the story

Telling this familiar story gives the whole group a shared experience and focus. It allows you to use gestures, voice and facial expression as well as interact with the children. Introduce one or two simple props and use these when telling the story – for example, a bag with five beans or two eggs to demonstrate numbers.

> ### Involving children
>
> *Who do you think this bag belongs to?*
>
> *What do you think can be done with these objects?*
>
> *Have you ever seen such objects before? Where? Can you tell their shape?*

Becoming involved

Teacher's role:

❖ Introduce the role-play area – the giant's castle – and a linked place such as the farmers' market.

Discuss with the children the size of different objects and compare with normal-sized objects. You could suggest putting together a collection of large- and small-sized objects, focusing on length, weight and volume.

Whose castle do you think this is? Can you explain why you think that?
Who lives here? How do you know?
What might happen here? Who will come here?
When you play in here, which character do you want to be? What will you do?

❖ Together with the children, act out climbing a magic beanstalk: instead of arriving at the giant's castle, you arrive somewhere else. Draw maps and pictures of this new place.

❖ Provide a range of measuring materials and invite children to help measure the distance across the room. Together make a long beanstalk (you could use crêpe paper leaves attached to a washing line) and suspend it 'growing' across the room.

At the end of the session, invite the children to be giants and discuss what has been happening in the castle today. Encourage children to respond using a 'giant's voice'. They could tell their stories sitting in a giant chair or standing on stage blocks to raise them up higher than everyone else.

Observations and assessment

Do children

- describe events in the correct order?
- compare various objects with regard to height and size?
- use a range of appropriate vocabulary?

Discussion time

What did the giant do today? Did he have any visitors?
Why does the giant need to wear such large shoes?
I wonder if the giant can see different things to us?
How long did it take Jack to climb the beanstalk?
If he started climbing in the morning, when do you think he'll have reached the top?
What other animals could lay a golden egg?

Let's do maths!

❖ Trace one of your hands on a piece of paper. Write the guess of how many beans fit in your hand on the paper. Count the beans you put on your hand.

❖ Fill up an egg box with enough eggs for the giant to eat.

❖ Do an audit of the giant's castle so that he will know if anything is missing.

❖ Plant some beans in a jar and count how many days before they sprout.

❖ Draw some giant footsteps in the outdoor area and follow to see where the giant was going.

Small-world and story-box play

You can explore the *Jack and the Beanstalk* story further with small-world toys, a story box or puppets.

Suggest that the giant cannot count very well and encourage the children to use the puppets to model counting the beans and eggs for the giant.

Create an indoors room in a small box. Contents might include: play people, animals, table, chairs, plates, spoons, pot, bag.

You can also transform the story box into a garden, using compost, plants, dried beans, plants, miniature watering can and gardening tools, play people and animals.

The Great Big Enormous Turnip

> **Maths learning**
>
> Describing, explaining and predicting
>
> Counting
>
> Comparing height and size
>
> Putting things in order of size
>
> Using the vocabulary of sequencing

The Great Big Enormous Turnip is a Russian folk tale, retold famously by Alexei Tolstoy. It is a story of the succession from largest to smallest, from old man to tiny mouse, who succeed in pulling a gigantic turnip from the ground. The twist in the tale is that the tiny mouse makes the difference to the final pull that extracts the turnip. The main opportunities for mathematical discussion are putting things in order of size and in sequencing events.

Setting it up

Children can enact the story themselves in a large space with simple headbands to show which character they are playing. Be prepared to observe whether children follow a repeated sequence of events, as in the story.

Role-play area and props:
Headbands for each of the characters (this could include one for the turnip); a large object to move (such as a bag of sand or a large pumpkin) which will require children to work collaboratively to solve the problem of how to move it; a large turnip (or carrot, potato or cabbage).

Getting started

Start with
* telling or reading the story

Re-enact the story in the outside area. Invite individual children to take the part of each character, wearing a simple badge or headband. One child could also be the 'turnip' that jumps up when they hear the 'tiny little mouse' join in. As they take part, ask the children to make themselves tall, small, tiny, and so on, to show how the sequence of characters gets smaller and smaller through the story. Suggest this as a way of remembering the sequence: the next person or animal is smaller than the last.

Involving children

I wonder how we can pull up this turnip from the sand?

Have we got a little mouse which would like to help?

Can you think of any other animals to help pull out the turnip?

Becoming involved

Teacher's role:
Introduce the props – the headbands.

❖ Discuss the story and the order of events with the children. Invite children to become characters in the story and to tell the story between them. You could invite a group to act out the story, leaving out one character. See if the rest of the group can say who is missing.

Who tries to pull first? Who will be next? Who are you going to ask to help you now?
Which character do you want to be? What will you do?
I wonder why the tiny little mouse helped the turnip come up?

❖ Introduce the small-world play. Support the children in retelling or developing the story, using the props and commenting on their size.

I wonder who helped after the dog?
How many characters do you think it took to pull out the great big enormous turnip?
Which is the smallest creature that will help?

At the end of the session, invite children to tell the story with all the characters they have found.

Let's do maths!

* Organise one or two kilos of turnips to be sorted by size or any other way children suggest.

* Suggest children use lining up as a length measuring device: *How far can we stretch if we hold hands with our arms straight? How far does the line reach if we stand one behind the other?*

* Set up a display of the smallest (or largest) things children can find.

* Ask children to close their eyes and identify different vegetables by shape.

Observations and assessment

Do children

- predict a sequence of events?
- put things in order of size?
- use a range of appropriate vocabulary?

Discussion time

Who did the old man call to? Who came after the little girl?
How can we put all these characters in order, from tallest to shortest?
I wonder if they could have pulled out the turnip another way?
How long do you think it took them to pull out the turnip?
What do you think they did with the turnip?
Which character did you most like to be? Why?
Who could the tiny little mouse call on to help if they still couldn't pull out the turnip?
Suppose a lioness comes to help, too. Where does she come in order?

Small-world and story-box play

Children reconstruct the story, using small-world materials and burying a turnip in a sand tray to be scooped out with a strainer or colander.

Children could also make up their own sequence for the story. Share one or two of these with larger groups of children and see if together you can all retell their story, remembering the invented sequence.

Who came after the cat? Where shall we put the goat?
Who is the first person to pull? Who is the last?
Who is the largest person? Who is the smallest?
I wonder what happened next?
How many characters are there in your story?

Fantasy role play

"There is no activity for which young children are better prepared than fantasy play."

Vivian Gussin Paley

Fantasy play provides a means of integrating social, emotional and intellectual growth. In relation to a role-play scenario, 'fantasy' refers to any play contexts that arise out of children's heads: heroes, goodies and baddies, monsters, witches and sorcerers, explorers, and so on. Such fantasy play often involves putting on cloaks and rushing about, or becoming a superstar with a 'microphone' or dance shoes.

Magic, too, features strongly in fantasy play. Children can reach a magical place by going on a magic carpet ride or meeting a magical person such as a wizard who whisks them off to a far-away land or a fairy godmother who grants wishes.

Fantasy play and pretend play are crucial aspects of role play. Leaving reality behind enables children to explore possibilities and look for fantastic solutions. Fantasy play has the potential to be more creative, more dynamic and more open-ended than role play linked to books, stories and real life. Children involved in fantasy play can, with sympathetic intervention, use more elaborate stories with a higher level of narrative structure and a greater degree of problem solving.

However, if such play is to become a valuable resource for mathematical learning, it is necessary to offer some structure as well. We need to observe how much reference is made to the mathematical props we have included as the children play: which children are making use of them? What are they interested in doing? We can then plan to ask questions such as: "How long will it take to fly there?"; "Is the monster much taller than you?"; "At what time do you think you can rescue the princess/catch the burglars?/perform the ballet?"

Further structure can be provided by creating characters and setting up the role-play area and choosing props together.

Adult input is important, but it is necessary to balance the imposing of adult ideas with giving children freedom to explore their own.

What's the maths in fantasy play?

As even superheroes need to make arrangements, receive and give directions to the trouble spot or make an emergency telephone call, there will be plenty of opportunities for mathematical learning experiences.

Numbers and the number system

Count, read, compare and order numbers:

I need to call for help ... This is the number I have to dial ...
What's the magic number? How many wishes do we need?
How many princesses are there?

Calculations

Combine groups of objects and take some away:

How many of us will fit in the space rocket? What if we add another two?
Has the tooth fairy left the same for everyone?
I wonder if there are enough dinosaurs.

Problem solving and using and applying

Sort and match objects, make choices and justify decisions:

Do we need more? Have we got enough? How can we find out? Are you sure about this?
How will you get to the bottom of the sea?
What will you do down there ... first ... next?
What do we do if the pirates catch us first?

Measures

Use the language of time, weigh objects, compare size and weight:

What time were you supposed to be there? Can you come and help in half an hour?
What can your monster lift?
How tall are you? How tall is the giant?
How long will you be away for?

How much water does the witch need in her cauldron?
Is that bag of moon dust heavier than this bag of moon rock?

Shape and space

Describe shapes, make patterns and give directions:

Can you describe this shape?
Why do you think it looks like a diamond?
What could you fit next in that pattern?
Where do we go next? Is that in the right direction?
Do we need to fly left or right?
How will you find your way back?

Fantasy themes

Goodies and baddies, heroes and superheroes, monsters and giants

The main feature of themes based on these
characters is usually something scary or
surprising happening, which is (or is not, as the
case may be) sorted out by a hero figure. It is
a concrete way children deal with abstract
concepts like hope and fear, good and bad,
kindness and cruelty.

'Wolf' and 'giant' themes which also occur in
traditional tales are taken a step further in
fantasy play.

Imagine I am Spiderman and I came and
rescued you ...
Can your monster run extra far?
I am the wolf, and I'm going to eat you all up. No, you're not! I am going
to chop you with my axe.
What size sandwiches do giants eat?

Power, control and relationships

The main feature of these is the exploration of events familiar to the
child and a familiar setting, often the home, where abstract concepts
such as safety, friendship, love, jealousy, kindness and cruelty can
be explored.

I'm the fairy queen. It's my wand, and I'll magic you.
I'm getting the knives and forks out for dinner. Let me see how many do

we need ... Wolves hate dinner. The wolf will just have to do as I say and eat up the soup.
He can eat three bowls. Or maybe five.
Pretend we're sisters and we lived together.
How long have we lived in the same house?
Pretend you're my mummy and I am your baby ...

Journeys

Space journeys or journeys to imaginary places often emerge from the role-play area and can be both familiar and fantasy. Abstract concepts such as fear, excitement, safety and danger are all encountered on journeys, short or long.

5, 4, 3, 2, 1 – blast off to the moon!
Look! There are palm trees, pyramids and sand below us!
This is a dark tunnel – but there's a circle of light at the end of it.
How far down into the centre of the earth are we going?
Look, this is the monster's footprint. How big must the monster be?

Entertainment

Themes that revolve around entertainment – music, ballet, opera, theatre, film and television – are equally popular.

Pretend we're disco singers and we've got the microphone.
How many tickets does the whole family need?
Let's all number the tickets for the seats.
How long does this performance last?

Maths learning
Describing, explaining and predicting
Counting
Ordering events
Comparing distances
Comparing duration
Comparing size and shape
Using the vocabulary of position and direction
Using the vocabulary of shape and space
Problem solving

Setting it up

A fantasy role-play area is more about enriching the environment for fantasy play than it is about building a particularly themed place, so raise children's awareness by creating an area for pretend play, a starting point for getting kitted up for whatever the children are exploring.

To start fantasy play, it often helps for the group to have a magical object such as a large conch shell, power beads or a magician's hat that, when held or worn, bestows magical power. Of course, sometimes a fairy godmother or the holder of a wand can perform just such a service!

Another magical conveyance could be a carpet or a special chair which, when seated on, will take children to wherever they wish to be.

Fantasy props:

Hats, bags, glittery necklaces, shawls, cloaks, fabrics such as velvet, muslin, silk and gold lamé; magic wand, conch shell, power beads; bubble mixture, gold dust, sequins, glitter, coloured water, rubber swords, glow sticks, masks, feathers; space equipment such as computer keyboards, calculators, headphones and walkie-talkies; cardboard boxes for building a rocket, castle or haunted house.

Becoming involved

Teacher's role:

Engage in pretend play in a low-key manner as a reserve player rather than a chief character. Make sure that the action is centred on the children and is child-initiated, so follow the children's plan rather than a previously worked-out plan of your own. 'Going with the flow' is a good rule for participating in children's fantasy play as the structure of play can change from one minute to the next. Remain flexible!

In fantasy play, part of the teacher's role is to offer new words and extend children's vocabulary: "Have you decided to use the hexagons to make space badges?" To suggest resources: "I wonder if the calculator would help you work it out." Involve children in making rules about superheroes play: "We won't run across anybody else's game"; "We'll be kind heroes, and we are careful when we're flying into space." To act as a messenger: "We need a princess to find out the missing number."

When children are in role, ask for their support in showing other children how to do something:
Can you show Lily how to count to five before she jumps off the bench?

Look for opportunities to explore and extend children's knowledge, both during and after play:
Do you know what to do when Superman's cape gets tangled up in the tree branches? Which number would you call to get help?

Invite a group of children to sit on the magic carpet and fly somewhere. Model a journey description yourself first, then encourage children to give descriptions themselves.

Use the outdoor area to develop children's spatial awareness and rope off a space where children can safely run, swoop and twirl. Provide cloaks and crêpe ribbons so that they experience speed and space as they move. Occasionally build narrow pathways and resource with tunnels.

At the end of the session, invite children to sit in a circle and talk about what they most liked about the fantasy play.

Observations and assessment

Do children

- use the props appropriately?
- interact with each other?
- get thoroughly involved in the fantasy role play?

Discussion time

What did Superman do today?
What happened next? Why do you think that happened?
How many people did he rescue?
How long did you fly to the moon? What stars did you see on the way? Were they all the same shape?
How did you find your way back?
What character would you like to be next? Can you explain why?

Small-world and story-box play

After the fantasy or pretend play has run its course, providing small-world figures and a reduced scenario such as a large tray or covered table top will prompt children in the action recall.

Alternatively, children can use a story box to recreate a particular fantasy scene. The contents of the box will depend on the theme they have chosen.

Let's do maths!

- Make a superhero cloak covered with stars, circles and other shapes.
- Count how many passengers will go in the rocket and write down their names.
- Draw a space map.
- Make tiaras and magic wands.
- Make witch's potions, using differently coloured water or coloured sand.
- Make a magician's hat by cutting a circle up the radius, folding it over and gluing it together.
- Use different-sized cardboard tubes and cylinders to make lasers.
- Provide a magic counting conch shell which gives magic counting ability to the holder.
- Hide a soft toy that needs locating and rescuing. Relay message clues, using positional information such as: "He says that he needs rescuing from somewhere low down next to the climbing frame."
- Number seats and tickets for a show.

Chapter 7

Extending maths learning

"Like the crest of a peacock, so is mathematics at the head of all learning."

An old Indian saying

We know that children's learning often takes off in a completely different direction to that we had planned, and nowhere are there more possibilities for this than in role play.

We need to plan the activities and rehearse the possible directions play may take based on our detailed knowledge of children's interests. We need to be ready to intervene and suggest mathematical problems in order to take the learning to the next level.

Identifying discussion starters is a good way of stimulating mathematical conversations. Present the maths in a way that is meaningful to children. Talk about what children are doing to help develop mental images. Rehearse solutions and think out loud.

On the whole, children spend more time in 'pretend talk' with their peers than with adults. But as adults working alongside them, we can support children's developing mathematical ideas not by organising and directing them but by prompting, guiding and engaging children in discussion. In pretend play, we must remember that the agenda belongs to the children. It is only fair to engage in talk within the context of their fantasy. It is during discussion that gaps in children's understanding become evident and co-working together shows its potential.

Indeed many focussed maths discussions take place between bouts of play as children have had time for reflection.

Some lengthy conversations can develop from the following discussion starters:

I wonder if ...

How shall we organise ...?

How can we find out ...?

How can we share equally ...?

Does anyone have a good idea about ...?

Would finding out how many there are be helpful?

I'm not sure if that's the same length as ... What do you think?

What would happen if ...?

Resourcing for learning

We want children to experience challenge based on a real-life purpose, and, often, what affects the quality of learning is the quality of resources we provide and their relevance and ability to support and extend children's learning.

Using numbers in context

Counting and working with number words can be used in almost every role-play area, and using prompts such as "I wonder how many we will need" and "I wonder if six will be enough" will always get everybody counting out and estimating.

Children's own symbols hold a lot of meaning for them. As well as providing printed numerals, create opportunities for children to draw and write their own numbers. For example, they can make their own price labels in the shop, write notes for a telephone number message board and make telephone number lists. To extend real-life play in a shop scenario, make batches of cheques and credit slips for children to fill in.

Set up a baker's shop and price bread, cakes and buns, use real money, put up a price list and use a visit to the shop as an opportunity to sing 'Five little buns in a baker's shop'.

Use bun trays and put a salt dough biscuit in each space. Count how many you need to fill the whole tray. Sometimes count the spaces and sometimes count the biscuits. Ask questions such as: "Have we got enough biscuits to fill up the tray?"; "How many more biscuits do you need?"

Have a birthday party in the home corner and include candles, cakes and birthday banners.

Calculating

"How many altogether?" and "How many will you give each teddy?" are questions that encourage calculations. Include also "Let's pretend to give everyone more" or "Let's pretend some pennies got lost and take some away" and the mathematical conversation rises to a new dimension.

Measures

We can plan to involve children in comparing weights, lengths and capacity in their role play, and we can make it more authentic by involving children in choosing the measuring resources themselves.

Every shop, supermarket, post office, market stall or takeaway scenario offers weighing possibilities. Use bucket balances to weigh potatoes, parcels and books; use rulers, tape measures and string to measure the length of various objects.

Shape and space

Explore shape and space by resourcing the shop or supermarket with an assortment of empty bags, boxes and shopping trays to be filled. Do an audit of the shop and look at how different-shaped boxes and tins stack up. Some market stalls sell fruit and vegetables by the bowlful, so collect a range of different-sized plastic bowls and investigate how much each bowl will hold. Together decide which bowl to fill up with potatoes or tomatoes.

Developing the role-play drama with maths in mind

Role-play areas do not need to be lavish productions: they can be just as effective as small areas that only last a couple of days to a week. All young children will benefit from having access to a moveable role-play area such as a pretend travelling theatre, or you can set up a drama centre, using stage blocks and a props basket, and retell stories. 'Theatres' can contain all the elements of a good role-play area such as props, dressing-up outfits which need to be nothing more complicated than a hat or a bag and the possibility of rehearsing being someone

else. Then add a mathematical twist of a problem to solve or an investigation to be carried out or choose a part of the story to engage with.

In the traditional tale of *Cinderella*, for example, some of the maths can be introduced by having a selection of different-sized shoes to try on. Children are always interested in their own and others shoes. Take advantage of this and set up a 'Before the ball' shoe shop, where children can choose and buy shoes using cheques, credit cards or notes. After the ball, it could become a 'Shoe Agency' where customers can return shoes, receive refunds and buy more shoes.

On another occasion, you can encourage the children to sort the shoes into different categories. The sorting will reflect the experiences of the children: "These shoes are red"; "These shoes are for rainy days"; "These shoes are for dancing." Make sure that some of the shoes are too small to get on and resource with some really large boots that are almost impossible to walk in. Sort the shoes by colour, by size, by purpose: "These shoes are for hot days, these ones are for winter weather."

Match the shoes in pairs and talk about left and right. Arrange shoe collections in order of size. Use words such as 'smaller' and 'larger' and ask questions such as: "Can you find a shoe that matches this one? Can you find a shoe larger/smaller than this one?" Provide measuring tapes and foot measures as well as a foot-measuring machine constructed from recycled materials.

The table opposite will give you some further ideas for introducing maths into the role-play area.

Maths development	Context	Provision
Recognising numerals	Technology in the home	TV with number dial, microwave, scales, telephones, clocks, dials, calculators, computers, electric meter, electric mixer with numbers on dial, oven, radiators with numbers on thermostat, iron
	Labels and signs	Front door numbers, magnetic numbers stuck on fridge, clothes and shoe-size labels, telephone numbers by the telephone, shopping lists in the kitchen, prices on food packets
	Tools	Measuring spoons and jugs, thermometers, medicine bottles
	Printed material	Books and magazines, coins, credit cards, chequebooks, stamps, greetings cards, envelopes, diary, telephone directory, TV listings
Numbers to show how many	Labels	Number labels for tidying implements and equipment and to show how many children can play, recipe cards showing the number of cups or spoonfuls needed
Counting opportunities	Mealtimes	Plates, cutlery, cups and mugs, pretend food, chairs, soft toys
	Dressing	Jackets, cardigans with buttons, pairs of socks, shoes and gloves, hats and soft toys
Shape	Furnishings	Fabric printed with shapes, cushions, table mats, saucepans, and so on, of different shapes
Space	Arranging furniture	New or different furniture for the home corner
Movement	Turning handles	Handles, dials, knobs, doors, windows, mincer, tin opener, baby food mill, salad spinner
Angles	Folding	Tablecloths, tea towels, towels, clothes
Size	Dressing dolls	Different-sized dolls, different-sized clothes, furniture

Books, books, books

Books are an invaluable source of inspiration when planning for role-play sessions in combination with mathematics. Check out what's available in your school library, using this list of classic and modern books as a guideline.

Real-life scenarios		
Mrs Lather's Laundry Alan Ahlberg Puffin, 1981	The Lathers decide to wash everything.	Time
The Great Pet Sale Mick Inkpen Hodder & Stoughton, 1998	All the animals are for sale. Which ones can be bought for 50p?	Money
I am TOO Absolutely Small for School Lauren Child Orchard Books, 2003	Explores the mixed feelings children have when they start school.	Counting
Alfie's Feet Shirley Hughes Red Fox, 1997	Alfie stamps in puddles with his new boots.	Left and right
Storybooks and picture books		
Where's My Teddy? Jez Alborough Walker Books, 1992	A picnic in a forest turns scary.	Size
Who Sank the Boat? Pamela Allen Puffin, 1988	The animals all want to go on a boat trip.	Comparing sizes and weights
Katie Morag Delivers the Mail Mairi Hedderwick Red Fox, 1997	Uses the context of a post office and journeys.	Positional language
Bunny Money Rosemary Wells Puffin, 2000	Max and Ruby go shopping for a present for granny.	Money
Traditional tales		
Jim and the Beanstalk Raymond Briggs Puffin, 1973	A boy named Jim meets an unhappy giant.	Sizes and measurement
Farmer Duck Martin Wadell/Helen Oxenbury Walker Books, 2006	Classic tale of a duck that lives with a lazy farmer.	Data handling
Who's been Eating My Porridge? Nick Ward Scholastic Children's Books, 2003	A cast of fairy-tale characters look for the porridge monster.	Trails and positional language
The Three Little Wolves and the Big Bad Pig Eugene Trivizas/Helen Oxenbury Egmont, 2003	Role reversal: the pig takes over from the wolf.	A pop up story book with a focus on problem solving
Fantasy role play		
Man on the Moon Simon Bartram Templar Publishing, 2004	The diary of a moon man.	The vocabulary of time
The Night Pirates Peter Harris/Deborah Allwright Egmont, 2005	Adventures with a group of girl pirates.	Measurement
Room on the Broom Julia Donaldson/Axel Scheffler Macmillan Children's Books, 2001	An affable witch tries to solve her space problems.	Counting
Mess Monsters in the Garden Beth Shoshan/Piers Harper Meadowside Children's Books, 2005	Manic monster mayhem outdoors.	Shape and space

Some final words

Young children are powerful thinkers and problem solvers when they play, and mathematics can provide a strong context for developing positive learning dispositions. We can try to harness these by exploring the mathematical possibilities of what could be termed loosely 'playing without toys' and, instead, making things up and using imagination which is so relevant to mathematics.

We could ask ourselves why it is that people can remember lessons such as English and History. Perhaps it has to do with the fact that they tell stories and that much of the teaching has a story attached. Stories can be true as well as fictional: we tell stories of our lives daily as we recount what happened and what was said to us. Attaching a story to our maths may make the mathematics more memorable for our children, and stories have ends that resolve the problem at the heart of the story. This structure fits mathematical problem posing and solving perfectly.

So, whatever the real-life scenario, storybook, picture book or fantasy image, role play provides young children with a natural way of learning maths by stimulating their minds and letting them explore the world of maths at their own pace, creating a sound foundation for maths learning.